# Drawn To Dark Things

Michael Wade Johnson's

# Drawn To Dark Things

Drawn To Dark Things



**www.facebook.com/Micwj**
**Email at: Micwjohnson@aol.com**



**All photos from the author's private collection**

**Layout and Design by Michael Johnson**
**Proofread by Marcie Copass (thanks pook)**

# No Names
(Nameless dysfunctional children)

I use people for art
Is that wrong?
I want you in my life
To inspire me
I'll muse a few ideas
Out of you
Then kick you to the
curb
Sorry but no
I do not
Want you for
Love, affection, companionship,
Time, money, or sex
I just want you
For the art.

What I want to accomplish
With my remaining days:
Nothing really.
Give or take.
Left my ambition at the door
Want to be known
Yet want no one to know me
Embracing the chaos
Knowing security is fleeting
One day at a time
What tomorrow holds
Is a mystery that unwinds itself
As I sit back
Taking it all in.

Sometimes it comes down
To money or happiness
Which will you compromise?
Which will be sacrificed
To propel the other forward?
Will you forgo the chance at contentment
In order to gain monetary wealth?
Regale all the loss of individuality
To have conservative stability?
Or can you risk financial power
In order to like your occupation
And/or position in life?
Maybe you are one of the fortunate
Ones to have both
But remember, most of us are not.

Bought a stripper a drink
Last night
Paying for a little bit of
A woman's time
Not an unusual hobby
Quite a common ritual in fact
Woman play men
In every aspect
Although seen and recognized
Keep playing and playing
An unwinnable game

A stripper in a bar
Might be the most honorable find
At least the terms are already defined
Wants are blatantly obvious
From both sides
Why can't they all be
That straightforward?

I want to make you shake inside
Tremble with warm infatuation
Yet the truth is
I'm the boringest man alive
Total snoresville
Bound to live a very short life
So I want to get to the point
As quickly as I can

An impression upon you
That's the goal
Change you for the better
In some way
Just can't get past the fact
That I'm so fucking lame
With no talent
Or cool tricks
Nothing up my sleeve
Down my socks
In my pants!
I'm a Goethe tragedy
In repeat
But hey, if you're into
That sort of thing…

I got the cutest girl's phone number
Last night
But I got drunk and fell into
The swimming pool
And fried my cell!
All programmed
And no memory
Data lost, not stored mentally
Curse you technology!

Tongues fondle
each other
in the dark
Wanted to make sure
you knew
who you were kissing
That's why
I asked
"Do you know
who this is?"

Nothing gives me
More courage
Than you
No medal of honor
Could ever surface this kind
Of bravery
You make me
The person
I want to be
Not the shell I hide in

An owed debt.

Been wanting a car crash
or a broken bone
That's how bad it's gotten
Just something…anything to
break up the monotony
Something to take me
out of the game
Cause I'm tired of playing
with the same ole rules
Time to switch it up
Time to take some chances
Been on the sidelines living safe
for far too long
Ready for the blindfold
Ready to see what I'm made of
New life begins now…or bust.

Sometimes I almost feel
Human
Almost like a human being
At the very least, a carbon copy of.
Usually I'm drunk off my ass
When this epiphany occurs
A fleeting glimpse of connection
Sharing the magic that is life
And then it's gone
A bookmark of better times

So I get too numb to feel
In order to show feelings
Whether real or drunk induced
Start talking loud, groping hard
A 180 turn
A different world
With no inhibitions
I like this world
Think I'll stay.

Gave up a salary
For a little bit
Of sanity
Was it a fair trade off?

Wanna see hell?
Get yourself a job
With a name badge
And a dress code
Nothing says happiness
Like conformity

Couldn't take it
I'm not the
"wear the same thing
as everybody, everyday"
type

Life is full of vast wonders
So much that one
Could never experience it all
So why tie up all your time
Miserable in survival mode

Ship never came
So I'm paddling out
To look for the motherfucker.

It's earth day
And I didn't wrap a present
No gift to show appreciation
To a dying world
A mother
Of nurturing nature
The only home I've ever known
Polluted and soiled
Corrupted by her inhabitants
What crappy tenants we are

No "I'm sorry for global warming"
Card to sign
No "Please forgive us for we know
not what we do to you" poster
No "Hey did we really cut down
that many trees?" button

…denial is funny.

I think we all have
An internal rhythm
That sets us apart
Something that drives us
To our destinations
Something we must emerge in
To ever embrace contentment
An internal voice
Some choose to ignore
While others can not bear the screaming
And spend their lives trying to silence
The sound.

Dreams uncoil
And submerse
Every concept
Ever had
Out of nowhere
There're scenes
Vivid, languid
You were there
Next to me
We kissed
Could feel
The warm
Nicotine breath
Woke up
Tasting it
Wanting it
Two people
Worlds apart
Dreaming together.

I'm in-between jobs
In-between fucks
In-between lives
In-between luck
Self-castration
Not humiliation
Assimilation
Is abomination
Won't ask for help
Won't ask for head
Won't be dependant
Won't live life dead
Annex me
From fantasy
And let me
Exist listlessly.

Saw a guy riding a horse
Pulling the reins
With one hand
And talking on a cell phone
With the other.

It made me chuckle.

You say
"Grow up, take some responsibility,
credit for your actions"
Yet you are one of the most immature
People I know
A fake fickle fucking plan
A major mockery mangling me
I read you
Before I ever cracked you open
You've reinforced my every intuition
Don't need you, never needed you
To save my hairy ass
A fellow in distress?
Then, now, and always
Calling me a child – how ironic
Are you the one shattered?
Crying all alone and suffocating?
NO…NO…NO
You overplayed that dramatic role
As I snickered from
Behind the curtain
You are the ghost town
I am the ghost
Just passing through
Forever haunting, forever haunted.

Morning eye crust
Stretching arms and imagination
Chocolate Éclair for breakfast
Cup of mango orange juice
Early 60's soundtrack
To prolong complete revival
Sun glares unabashedly in window
Mental roller coaster has begun
Eyelids rubbed yet still unfocused
Turn on the cool water
And within minutes
Irish Spring awake
Alert yet still exhausted
Too much rendering to shadows
Giving in to nocturnal urges
To ever grip this normal routine
Dawn will always be my dusk

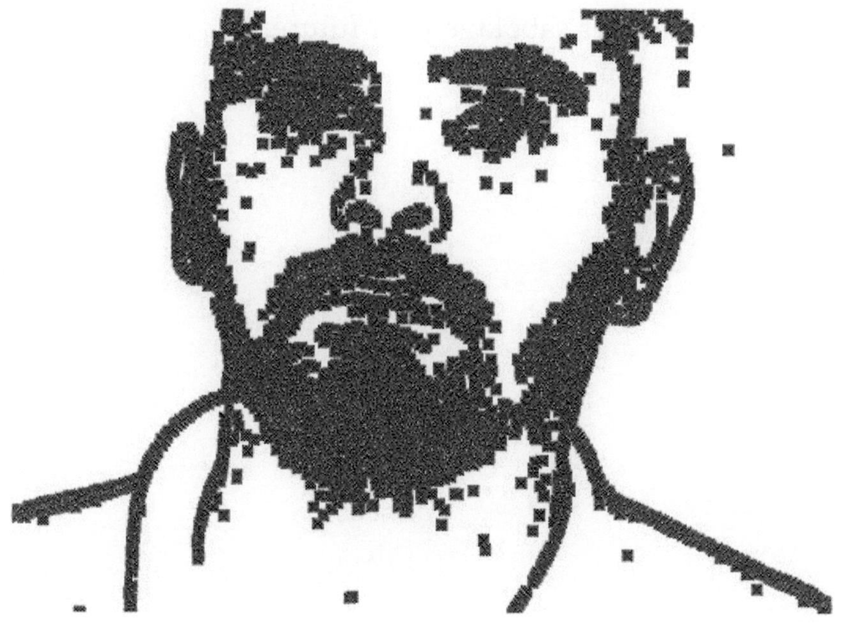

Compared you to the world
I know
Every girl that's ever come my way
Every inflection of voice
Your timing, your eyes
Your words, your moves
You
An unfair opportunity
To present yourself as original
And as a genuine portrait of self

Saw only imitation and reminders
Apprehending all forward advances
Culminating in a fierce stalemate
Caged like a cell mate
Until I could never be your mate

Moral: learning and taking notes from the past can sometimes sabotage your future.

Searching, highest highs to lowest lows
Streets, stone, trees, and meadows
Trying to find my voice
As if there was any choice
Hopefully this sweep around
The voice will finally be found
And contain no southern drawl
That has plagued me all along
Growing up in backwoods KY/TN
Thus my fate has always been
Family never saw behind the curtain
Myself, got a few peeks in for certain
And I can only hope what my kids
    and grandkids will do
Rip that son-of-a-bitch off the rod
    and then walk right through.

What happened in that room?
4 walls
3 lamps
2 beds
1 night
Suddenly came the dawn
Attitudes changed
Forever altered
Actions taken
In inebriation
Free spirited
Consented and enjoyed
Now guilt-laden
Spoken about in silence
By the inactive reactions
This day forward
Will be affected
Will be centered around
1 night
2 beds
3 lamps
4 walls.

I'm a GenXer
Does that mean
I have no work ethic?
Maybe
Am I less self-involved
Than the baby boomers?
Possibly
No respect for authority?
Could be
My generation did invert
Many traditional customs and ideals
So what did that leave the neXters?
A rebellion back to the old norms
Cyclical culture. Enjoy.

Those who are fat, old, ugly, or male
Shouldn't smoke

Only beautiful skinny females
Can pull it off
Make me want to do some "damage"

Must be a fetish
Don't really like the scent
But seeing a gorgeous
Sexy young woman
With an oral fixation
Does it for me every time

Puff away ladies
You may be banned from
Restaurants, stores, homes,
Airplanes, clubs, and other restricted areas

I'll never ban you from my fantasies.

I've been deleting you all day
All week
Therapeutic and evocative
An official sendoff

Reread everything of course
Trying to find reasons, hints,
And understandings.
An abysmal examination

One last hurrah
Through your many names
And your many moods
And your poetic mulch

All of the "you are my everything's"
And "forever" blah blah's
An instinctual façade
Time was bound to expose

Once the virtual is finished
Move on to the material
Leave only mental preservation
This sideshow project is over.

There were a few mornings
Waking up in strange places
Faint recollection of the night previous
Mostly tidbits to a much larger story
That will be told and reenacted
By companions
Nights when liquid got spilt
And carpet got a vomit bath
And clothes came off
And bruises were made
And opinions were boldly stated
And dancing became an option
And socializing was the game
I stumblingly played.

If I could
I'd watch horror movies
All daylong
To avoid the real horror
That is my life
Give me a Rob Zombie world
And I'll be at peace
Hanging out with Billy and Mandy
Isn't as grim
As working a full time job
Rather confront Jason, Freddy, Leatherface
And Michael Myers
Than confront mere mortals on a regular basis
I'd rather listen to the screams of scream queens
Than the blandness of silly drama
Give me blood, gore, evil, and whores
Anytime over duties, appointments, responsibilities, and chores
Give me horror
I'll take the tragedies and fantasies any day
This macabre reality is too scary to handle.

Trying to find that line
Between sexy cunt whore
And domestic sweet companion
Can we ever be happy
With a boring preplanned existence?
Will we ever regain sparks lost long ago?
Or can we find lasting comfort
in a constant supply of wild and carnivorous nights
with someone who is outgoing
and independently strong?
Must we choose the weak ones and settle?
Will the wild ones never be the faithful life partners
we can evolve with?
Can we ever have both enjoyment and stability
at the same time?

If I was young again
I'd care a lot less
I'd raise more hell
And nail every girl
Within range
And not hide my beliefs

…but I would either
be in jail or dead by now.

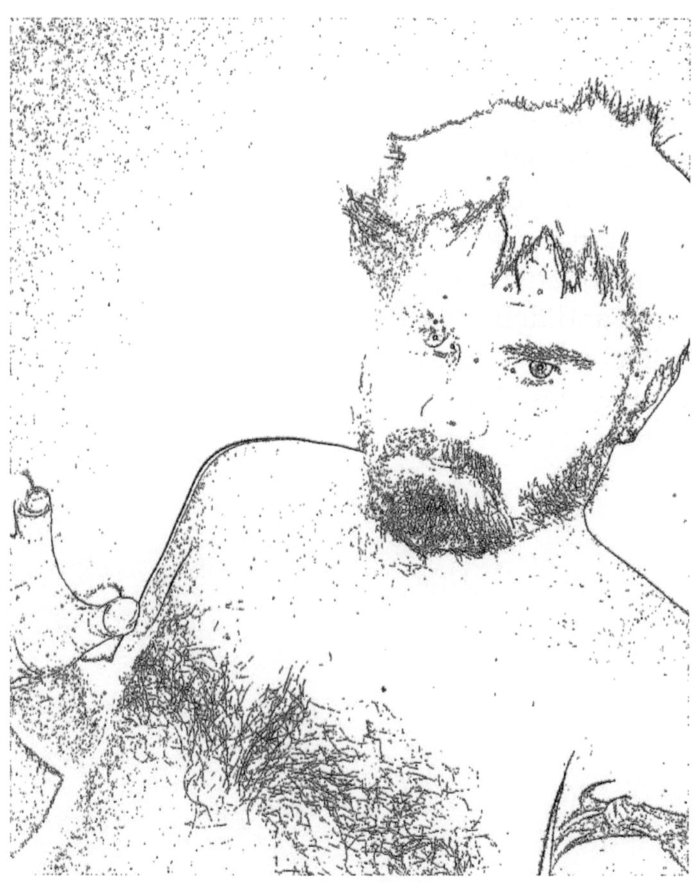

Too much vodka
Not enough sense
Push forward
Something that
Dares to destroy
That simple life
Mentality
That brick wall
Surrounding flesh
What might've happened
Might be
The craziest moment
That lives on
Forever more
Circumstantial
And DNA proof
Caught in a mystery
Unsure of anything
Drunk and delirious
Vodka be thy poison
Turning these lips
To stone.

Wake up around 4 or 5 pm
everyday
When most are going to happy hour
and / or home with their families
I'm wiping eye crust away
This nocturnal lifestyle
Can be daunting
at the most inappropriate times
Need an ear at 3 in the morning
but no one's awake
Want to hang out @ 5 am
what a ridiculous notion
Living like an inversion
Living in the night

You called me
The king of catnip
The majesty of maggots
An idiot

Mailed me the key
To your heart
Had to refuse
Return to sender

An ancient feeling
Even dinosaurs knew
And the first rocks
Colorful and shapely

You were a medic
Without proper bandages
To ever clean this wound
And sew up this soul

Knew from the get-go
Aiming in the dark
With a blindfold on
Miss or hit and run

Drew you a picture
A house with a view
Overlooking the sea
Crumpled in the garbage

Looking for a word
Not "I'm sorry"
Not "I told you so"
Maybe it's "goodbye"

Often get immersed in my own shit
So intensely that the smell eludes me
Like any artist, I give birth to creation
Like many mothers, I love my baby
But trying to step out
And look from outsiderland
Sometimes still fail to see
The flaws, the wrongs, the suckiness
Trying to define "true" art
Guess I am just lazy
Um, I mean a true outlaw
Not giving a fuck of opinions
Paying no mind of mindless masses
I'll do my own thing
Never gaining any acceptance
Forever building a losing legacy
My life, my art, my way
All critics can go to hell
So, everyone go to hell

Tonight the rockstar overdoses
And shoots himself in the bathtub
Just so you know

Time for a little
Inebriation initiation
A little trip to the
Land of intoxication
A place I know too well
A place you can recognize
By the sights and smell
May be just a left detour of hell
But it's still pretty damn swell
With the finest blend of lovely liquor
And ale
Yeah…
So let's have an
Inebriation initiation
An intoxication celebration
A way too drunk, to of thunk
About the puke and hangover coming up
A flipsy, tipsy, smashed up, bashed up
Kind of fun
Yeah...
An inebriation initiation
Over the top, under the influence
Beyond your control
Kind of vacation.

She spoke and wrote
of unconditional love
but she was full of shit
…hear me out…
She talked a good talk
and indeed
when she was hooked
she was as unconditional
as they come
But as for her
past relationship/ unconditional/
never ending/ always/ and forever
love
Nope, not true
The 24/7 connections
becomes not answering
calls or returning emails
Only an every now and then
"unconditional love"
One that suits her fancy
only when she sees fit
She has much to learn.

I understand why you
Pretty girls
Go for the
Preps, the jocks, "the men"
Sure, I mean, look
At us pussies
Geeks, dorks, poetic fags
Sensitive little mama's boys
Or maybe just EMOtional
Whatever the case
I mean yeah -
Muscled, rock brained males
Warriors who will crush and stomp
And hit and spit and drink beer
That's the panty wetters
Loving, artistic, talented smart guys
With a pent up sexual drive
And a complex to please -
Who the hell would want that?

She smoked Misti Ultra Light 100's
Listened to Shania Twain
Did excessive amounts of drugs
And fucked like a racehorse
Whatever that means
She left a Whatchamacallit
Candy bar at my doorstep
A "piece" offering
One I gladly accepted
Cause I was 20
And I was a motherfucker.

Woke up in a rush
With head spinning
And that smell
You know the one
Stripper smell
Jumped up wearing
Green strip club shirt
And nothing recalled
Total blackout
Retracing events
Bar hopping
Bellini pitchers
Long Islands
Yager bombs
Aftershock
Peach Snapps
More L.I.T.S.
Etc etc…
Then lap dancing
Stripper
Then
…nothing
Hours locked
From memory
Left with
That stripper smell
And a $110 receipt

The stake has been
driven in this cold heart
years ago.
Undersized, hard, and black.
Sunken in with hatred.
How dare you try and
Pull it out.
And revive that which
beats no more.
No sleeping beauty am I
but a monster
Who had monstrous things
done to him.
Miles away from innocence
Something lost so long ago
how can that be re-sparked?
I am certainly doubtful
But if anything could,
it would be your lips.

Obsessions that bounce off
The Richter scale
There have been a few
Started back in the 90's
Barrymore was the first
It was Mad Love at first sight
Then came S.M.G.
One or two screams and I was
A slain vampire
A dust pile in the wind
Drifting from one infatuation
To the next
With many other minor part players
My sights fixated on B-movie queens
Mundane spun her way into the screen
And seduction horror was never the same
Until Wuhrer raised some hell
Showing the benefits to being "deader"
Just when attention was adrift again
Shepis choked me into submission
With her wicked charm and talents
I am drawn to dark things
And drawn to those drawn
To dark things
And always will be.

Find that one can only
acquire the company of others
when delving in the vices
of self-destruction
and habitual substances.
Hear me out.
When I was straight edged
never involved in partaking
in man's many ruins,
No one wanted to hang around.
Only when I let it all go
Started a downward spin
Did I see the crowd
come to my door
Humans bonded by
depravity and the desire
to self-detonate.

Spoke to my ex-wife a couple nights ago. First time in a long time. Since I finally got tired of hearing her bullshit and went totally cold to her. Now there's that awkward silence that looms in the air. Anyway, she calls. Her grandmother has died and she wants to know if I'm coming to the wake. I tell her I don't think it's such a good idea. Her family hates me due to the villain she's made me out to be. A villain who destroyed the good morals and values of the pious angel. Yeah right. If only they knew. I liked her grandmother very much and respected her. She always treated me kind. But I hadn't seen her in years and I don't want to deal with the evil and snide comments from her family so I'll just pay my respects alone and in my own way. My ex may hate me forever for it but she was getting a good start on that anyway.

I'm not sure what to say without saying too much,
revealing the man behind the mask.
A rehashing of the caustic verbiage
that could entice or bore you to the core.
Life is messy as always and I find myself peering down
rabbit holes but never fully jumping in.
A neurotic paranoid with good reason.
I surround myself with those who seek to destroy me.
Maybe anyone would fit the bill, but the current
aficionados are hungry enough to accomplish the job. As
nihilist as ever, as alcoholic as ever, as vulnerable as ever.
Making mistakes like some make eggs: sometimes
scrambled and sometimes sunny side up.
A little more numb to the pain, without any painkillers.
If I knew the right words, I'd send them.
But for now hopefully this will suffice.

2:30 in the morning
Lost in a vacant vision of bewildered wonderment
Feel the buckle of my chaotic choices
The rain falls outside
Pounding rhythms out on the roof
Collapsing with a mental mirage
Life constantly brings the questions
Constantly brings the glimpse of glimmer
I stay in the dark, hiding from the light
Hiding from what's right
Getting drenched in the downpour
Softly glowing on flesh
Thinking of the bottles emptied
Of the desires whispered
The season ends, now begins anew
New patterns get formed in a fury
And with it new doors that are locked
Begging to be picked and entered
How long can a façade remain covered in veil?
Only the tedious table of time will tell…

Life is a confusing puzzle to piece
Putting everything together, trying to fit perfectly
But that seldom ever happens
Rephrase: that never happens.
Emotions run the game and fill the gaps
Ranging from heavenly to hellish.
But what's an abused reaction?
To charge everything to two slots (L/H)
To label everyone with a symbol of hope.
Life shouts out those demands
It comes with no manual.
Not write or wrong word play.
Just a mess to clean up in the morning
Rinse and repeat, all over again.
Feelings that no one can control
Run rampant over the mind fields.
One day all perception is changed.
Morality is a mockery
And sentimentality is infamy.
Owing nothing to the world
But the debt that's embraced.
Destined to end badly
As everything eventually does.
The puzzle gets reset.

Scary thoughts
Too much is felt
Too soon
Too unknowingly
Too uncontrollable
Is it real?
What is real?
How does she really feel?
A game or more?
Time spent for
A building of sorts
Stressful pleasure
Secrets hidden
Tasting forbidden
Worthy of measure
What plans has she
Of her and me?
A scheme or something else?
A casual thing
Or…growing?
These are things
I need knowing.

Isn't it funny
How you are
Friends with people
Merely because they
Reside in the same area
Or town as you
And when one of you moves away
It's like an instant disconnection
And disassociation
No need of the bond anymore
No need to pretend
The illusion erodes away
As disdain sets in
And reality becomes shockingly obvious
People are leeches, people
Beware of them all.

Not long after graduating high school
Got arrested
(taken "downtown", never incarcerated)
For possession of narcotics
(released on bond)

But the irony was,
I had never done drugs
Never sold drugs
Never had "possessed" drugs

By then I already knew
The injustice of judicial laws

One more coal for the fire.

My wonderful 4-door
Ugly white Mirage of a car
Isn't exactly a pussy magnet

I need a suped up sporty car
Or a big truck
I mean a really big truck

My friend used to own one
Grand in proportion and stature
Worked like a charm
Young ladies would line up
For a chance to ride

But I never had a big truck
So I never got the line of girls
But it's ok
Cause most of the girls
That dig that sort of thing
You wouldn't really
Want to bed anyway…um…right?

Spending time silly searching
Making meaning of mediocrity
Is like getting kicked
In the Gedan
Gonna take a few minutes
To recover from the sting
By all means, do your thing
Pick your fancy and your friends
And your nose all at once.
Stop and smell the sewer
Take candy from a call girl
You can't have your clit and
Eat it too (not in Zimbabwe)
Life is boxes of chocolates
But not Russell Stover
The Dollar Store kind
(mixed with ex-lax)
And there is no
Paradise by the dashboard light
No unskinny to my bop
No cherry to my pie
No twice to my shyness
There's only time to kill in between
To quote Billie Joe Armstrong:
"fill the void with, I don't care..."

Go to bookstores
You know what I mean
Looking for that tiny, tiny section
The section smaller than most
You know the one
The poetry section
Why is poetry not marketable?
All the shelf will contain is
Beowulf, Whitman, Poe, Shakespeare,
Maya Angelou, Frost, and Charles Bukowski
Not that Bukowski isn't great
Poe too
But where is the modern poet?
Where is the acceptance of today's scribblers?
A select few, maybe, sure
In a sea of millions
If poetry is dead
CNN should announce it
So we can put down these pens
Once and for all.

Books in a row
On the shelf
Crumpled money
On the desk
Bottle of Sangria
Cheap and finished off
Laptop blaring
In the bedroom
Death smiles
In the background
Beautiful whores
Dance the routine
Drama queens
Pout their lips
Actors act like
The action is real
Blood runs on
The metro-link
Some nights
Everything is perfect
Perfect gets antsy
Staying too long.

Watch doomsday
programs on TV
The forecast of
the deadly destruction
to dear planet Earth
Be it by nuclear fire
meteorite blast, the sun
or big bang part two
Shown quite often
mostly the History Channel
Watch these not
with faith beliefs
Alerting the public
with apocalyptic warnings
No
Watch these predictions
to reinforce the fact
that every action
performed on this planet
is inevitably futile.

From the get-go
as they say
Cliché but true
Those eyes did
a number on me
Drawn to the
darkness within
The effulgent surface
The veraciousness beyond
A craving
Like a pregnant lady
with the urge
for fried pickled sherbet flan
with spinach ice cream
- had to have it
to quiet the longing
Had to again and again
It's been a plight filled situation
A smoldering obsession
Tangent in discretion
Every movement exudes passion
with a touch of you all naughty
A hottie without being haughty
An image replayed constantly
You are my provocation, it's true
but I am too prosaic for you.

I have always looked younger
Than I am
In appearance.
When I was 18
People thought I was 15
When I was 21
People thought I was 18
When I was 25
People thought I was 21
At 30
People thought mid-twenties
But as I get older
Can see it catching up with me
Slowly but surely
The gray doesn't hide anymore
The wrinkles aren't few
Never really wanted to grow old
But the transition train ride
Is smooth
And I've already paid my ticket.

Times are tough
But we all live the good life
From here in this duplex
Fail to see the poverty
And the economical depressions
Watch "A Daily Show" for news
And Sci Fi for horror
Drink sparkling grape juice
Eat fruit from the mega-mart
And wither away
As bones turn to brittle
And hope turns to hang-ups
Vision goes bad
Hearing goes bad
Never step outside
Only to drive away quickly
No connection to the world
Go to a restaurant or café
To be surrounded by strangers
Feeling their presence
Heals the hurt from loneliness
By denying how incredibly
Alone we really are.

You say you enjoy it
More when I moan
Say it turns you on

I say when you moan
It makes me moan
Harmonious rhythm

We shouted it out
For everyone to hear.

I used to be a serial killer
Dropping a few bodies here and there
Always enjoyed the blood splattered everywhere.
Never used protection
Just went with the instincts
Felt the life in my hands
The god-like power I welded
Truly amazing rush.
Who did I kill, you ask?
Hookers? No
Homeless? No
Elderly? No
Couples? No
Babies …yes babies
I kill the unborn
I knock up tons of women
And force them to have abortions
Against their will if needed
Murdered too many too list
A totaled number
The Manson family would have envied
I am doing the world a favor
Come girls let me pop that balloon in your womb

p.s. this is a work of fiction. so don't profile me F.B.I., you bitches !

She wasn't wanting a permanent fix
Just something to get through the day
He wasn't planning for a pact substantial
Just something on the side
She widened her eyes
To the thought of contentment
With the image she'd held dear
He fought the resistance
To give in illogically
To an endeavor that left him breathless
Could they find salvation in each other's arms?
Were they destined to destruct in turmoil?
They entered a complicated and confusing game
Where there is no turning back.

Watching a Buffy DVD
Season one, disc one
Re-watching the episodes
From "Welcome to the Hellmouth"
All the way to "Chosen"
A repeated ritual
Sure, there are wars overseas
Out in the streets
In the bedrooms
Inside my head
Poverty and diseases
Spreading over decaying land
There's real evil to fight
Hard choices to decide
- rather not deal
A total wiggins
Need the BTVS
For a beautiful distraction
Plan an escape to Sunnydale.

Driving around in the middle of the night.
In sheer panic from every catastrophe
that could possibly occur.
This is what I miss the most
from the young and naïve days.
The connecting to others without caution.
Hell, I can't have a conversation with someone
these days without being paranoid of the backlash.
In the old blissful ways,
affection could be attached quite easily.
Now it's like getting into the NASA space station.
Security clearance and all.
Sparkle and fade forever, baby.

Never was in treatment
All through the years
Saw a few counselors
Took a few tests
Was recommended psychoanalysis
And prescribed medicine
Even electroshock therapy
Made a few calls to hot lines
Still yet never made it to the couch
Unleashing my demons to a pro
Even as self aware of the problem
Felt an internal force saying, "don't cop out"
So without the guidance and support
Trudged forward all alone
Survived over 15 years and counting
Battling an unseen enemy
Winning and losing to it
Whatever outcome may prevail
Was accomplished on my own terms
Without any enhancements

Yo, I'm a homeboy
That is to say
I stay at home a lot
Have always been this way
An inherited trait for sure
Remained home all through high school
Almost every long-term band I was in
Practiced at my house
Rather have friends visit me
Than the opposite
It's just the only place
I feel completely secure
Broken out of that shell a little
Not as primitive as I used to be
Can't deny that I still prefer
To be in the comforts of the sanctuary
Home is where the art is

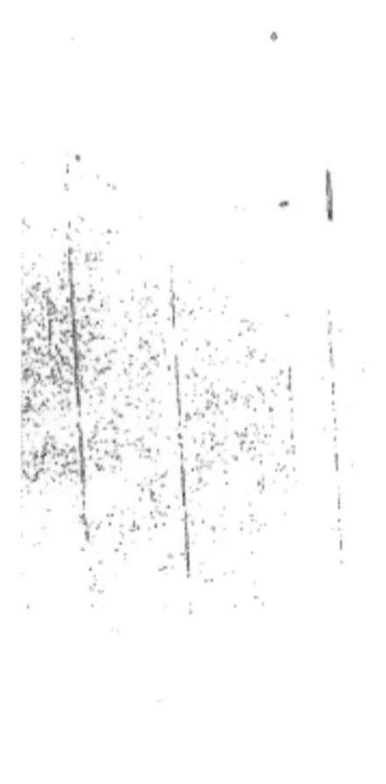

Can't believe until that night
I had no idea you were my enemy
Unsuspecting of it all
For ten years of revealing
My weaknesses and intimate details
It never registered
Until you let it slip
Told me what I really was
In relation to you
Might've never caught on
I'm glad you exposed it
Cause things will never be the same
See you for what you truly are
The only true player
In this competition game

My job: hacker

My mission: infiltrate the breaching of authorized
Personnel with clearance to detonate
The nuclear warheads in the Nevada desert

The progression: almost complete

The outcome: total destruction of a miserable
Spinning ball in space.

Generally I sit around, watch movies, listen to music, sleep, write a little here and there, and work on various artistic creations. Yet I get labeled from practical strangers. People who know me in passing. People I reveal little or nothing to. So they are led to assume that I'm a Satanist. That I'm a playa. That I'm a crystal meth dealer. WTF? That is absolutely ridiculous, so much that it's laughable. I don't have an altar, nor do I break tons of hearts. I don't do drugs, I don't sell them. People have whispered this my whole life. Like I must be a living embodiment of a stereotype. Then there are all the "friends" who perpetuate the bullshit even farther. The ones who smile in my face and pretend to care while going behind my back and starting these fucking rumors. Get tired of hearing it, one after another. I moved away and I'm still hearing shit from that hick town. Must I forever be their scapegoat? I fight to stay off the radar yet I always seem to be the topic of conversation. For the most part, I hate how fucking judgmental and hypocritical the human race is. Fuck you all, you pricks.

Go and fuck all
The beautiful women
You can

It won't change
How ugly you are
On the inside.

The brazen sad reality
Of it all is
That everyone's life
Eventually comes crashing down
We build up our relationships
Our immunities, our hobbies
Our health, our knowledge, our wealth
Our position in the kingdom
Merely to one day lose it all
Not probability, proven fact
Human spirit is an odd enigma
Constantly against the current
The enormous struggle to survive
To push the species forward
Not go the way of the dinosaur
Yet with no real continuation
No prize or trophy at the finish
A cold quiet grave of emptiness
Hollowed, nulled and voided
One of these days everyone
Will decide to sleep in and dream.

Can't explain to you
Everything I've wanted to
Can't tell you
Why a lot of writers lose their talent
After a while
Why musicians can be the same
Can't make you understand
That I have always been a hack
At every medium I've ever tried
That it worsens all the time
Can't make you see
That there is no importance in me
No significance for the outside world
A contribution of zero
There is nothing great about me
Can't get you to agree though
You see me in a different hue
Thank you for being you.
Amorous through it all.

This is it, last call
Last chance for a wake up call
You have a choice, can't have it all
One last round, one last call
This steamy ship's about t' take a fall

Here it is, last call
Last chance for a make up call
You have a sip yet want it all
It's your cue, your call
Make up ya mind b'fore I make a fall

Last call, last call
This is my last call.

A starving artist
Starving for art
For clout and venom
With movement momentum

Dry mouthed with hope
For kerosene soaked words
Letters that react
To the simplest actions

Feed all the scraps
The week old ideas
Devoured like delicacy
Lapping ankle high

Forever hungry for more.

* Are you my Dr Carl Von Cosel?

* **All consumers are consumed by the magic spell of commerce. Wake up zombies!**

* *When it comes to war, I'm a total hippie.*
  *Not that I'm unsympathetic. Just way too empathetic.*

* He spent the morning hours masturbating to a girl he just met via webcam. He had no idea she was a dude.

* *People posing: not a black sheep, just a sheep in black*

* **Eyebrows are the curtains to the soul**

* Learned from Kraven that once you reach the pinnacle, you put the shotgun in your mouth. Cause there is nothing left.

* *Life is an elaborate popularity contest, with my likeability completely faltered.*

* **Me – an idealistic voyeur; You – heaven replicated**

* Old man now, still no little critter at my feet. Does this make me shallow?

* **Slavery will always exist in this cruel plateau. It's like going to hell with your back broken.**

* Drain my modicum nest egg until it cracks.

# Named

(Titled, normal children)

## Sharing Showers

She tosses off the last article
of clothing attached to her

He cracks his neck and leans
forward in anticipation

She experiments with knobs
to find the perfect temp.

He holds out his hand
and clasps at descending H2O

She steps inward

He moves forward

She's entranced with the feel
that's crescendoing on her skin

His breath skips as she fills
up every possible thought

She is closing her eyes
as her pores get saturated

He is soaking up the moment
as his hair curls upward

She thinks of only him

He thinks of only her

**Sharing Showers** **(continued)**

Both are drenched

She steps out of the tub
and grabs a towel

The time is 11 p.m.

He steps off the sidewalk
and turns toward his apartment

As the rain drains from the clouds
in a stark dark sky

The time is 11 p.m.

## Cowboy Hats

Stopped in a neighboring town's Wal-mart
In the twilight hours
Went into the restroom/bathroom
Did I rest or take a bath?
No
Anyway
I went into the stall
And as I was unloading
Saw before me
The box of thin toilet seat covers
Someone had taken
A marker
And written on the box
"free cowboy hats"
I laughed so fucking hard
I thought I was going to vomit
I would have pissed myself
If I wasn't doing that already.

## Ismail Ax

a warning to the world :

there are time-bombs out there
you can't always hear the ticking
so warning signs?
well, a dark creative outlet
isn't a cause for stake burning
not every morbid writer is a killer
but maybe signs are prevalent more so
in things such as
physical response and emotional damage
which also aren't easily detected
to a causal observer

the truth is some people just snap
yes the ones deprived and outcast
are more susceptible
but anyone can be next
anyone.

## Trashing Treasure

You are the kind of girl
Doesn't stay on the market
Too long
Too cool, too easy on the eye
Too everything every man wants
A sensitive heart
Yet with sultry passion
A dark disposition from a sunny position
A creative soul searching for happiness
A miracle witnessed by common spectacle
And the sad irony, you are oblivious
Unbeknownst of this great power
The loveliest "ugly duckling"
A remarkable unshone star
Amidst the glory and the overrated
Yet more radiant than any around
What a gem to behold! To hold!
To share a connection
So how could anyone
With full mental capacity
And comprehension
Trash such amazing treasure?

## Wishes Happen To Be Horses Today

Dust gathers on last season's letters
Chalk residue tends to have a dry taste
Wind calls through the dancing elms
Thunderstorms high on radar scans

Time ticks harder with each passed second
Noticing the absence of what was
The brief whispers, a blink of fireworks
Astonishment not reserved for youth

Amidst the silent trauma of journey
Intangible twist lingers far too long
Wishes happen to be horses today
As carpet dreams become reality.

## My thoughts on Humans: their egotisms, fickleness, and predictability

It's funny, the more I go through life,
the more I see the same shit
Happening over and over again
People are so caught up in themselves, thinking they are
the greatest things ever
Bound and determined to shine
Well I've seen tons of these stars burnout
and dwindle to the ground
So easy to predict, it's almost sad

I'll be honest, I'm not great in any form.
I don't have wonderful ideas or anything
Like that
What I do have is passion and determination
And other leeches latch on to that
until they get to where they think they can stand
alone and survive without my drive and influence
Then they proceed to drop me like a boulder in the water
This shit happens every god damn time
While it's true, I may be hard to work with artistically
It mostly is due to the egotisms by these leeches
So they detach and go their merry little way
And without the perseverance they eventually fall and fail
Usually end up quitting or disbanding

So this is never a shock to me
Yet I continue to create these project endeavors
involving other humans
Which is my mistake entirely
But some things are hard to accomplish alone
That hard fact you will find out soon enough.

## Inanimate Objects Beware!

only so much
of this game
will be taken
this sly witty wordplay
poems from a nonpoet
slandering me
eventually i will pop
use letters as weapons
you really don't wanna get into a word fight with me
trust me...
better hang it up
and go be a superstar.

## Expendable All Are We

I like the idea of being easily replaced
Like knowing that there is nothing special
About me or within me
Reopens the awareness of one simple fact:
We are all expendable
The world turns on without breaking stride
We are what we are and that's it
Nothing less or more
All parts in a machine
Getting substituted when shown with wear
For better efficiency
Traded up and traded in
I don't feel the need to stroke my ego
Give myself super importance
I am matter…..that doesn't matter

## Gouge out your eyes

A color
A hint of suggestion
An afterthought of negativity
A hidden agenda
A simple insinuation
That can cloud judgments
Some textures aren't as
Transparent
Void of solidity
Tied to a stigmatism
A shade,
Set apart by a shade
A fraction of pigment
…come on people.

## Clusterfuck

Heart always clasps for
what the mind says it shouldn't

Logic and emotions
in a boxing match to the death

Complacency is the
holy grail of this era

Reason slaps feelings on the hand
and points a tisk tisk finger

Incompetent enough not to
carry out such complex details

Without making a decision,
a decision is made.

## Standing Coma

The point
T h e   p o i n t ?
Yeah, passed it a while back
Now swirly vision in overdrive
Staggering back to the booth
Order another vodka and sprite
Put it on the tab
Grin at the pretty girls
Go back to the bathroom
Piss, vomit, piss
Wash hands and dry
Limp out on the dance floor
Drink to the boogieing girls
Mind your own business
Keep on sipping
Smile and be friendly
Slurred speech
Dizzy
Wake up home
Wonder how the hell
You drove back.

## Ventilation Shaft

Will you ever
fucking grow up?
Stop fucking around
like a dickhead
Shave off this
thick insecurity
Quit feeling so
small and helpless
Do you have balls
or what?
Be a man for once
stubborn, hard, cocky
Don't go soft
in your old age
Time has come!

Umm…sorry, everyone
just talking to my penis

## When Pluto Was A Planet

Reminisce the past
For a better future
What went wrong
Was never conclusive

When Pluto was a planet
When the world was aligned
When your heart lie in my hand
When everything seemed right

Dig deeper dear
Remember these moments
Only the mind
Can backtrack the components

When Pluto was a planet
When global warming was a myth
When celebrities were stars
When you, I didn't have to miss

Now look how it all ended up down the line
We may have been un-advanced at the time
Still ignorance is a blissful frame of mind
When Pluto was a planet and you were mine.

## Star Boy

This letter has been a long time in the making. Been meaning to talk to you face to face and have this conversation. But I now have decided against it. In person isn't going to alter any circumstance. I am bothered by the constant stories and allegations I hear from our many connections. But you knowing I know will not change anything. It never has. This is who you are and I cannot shame you into taking a step in the opposite direction. So the choice comes before me: to accept you this way or distance myself forever. Both are difficult. We were together during the maturing years, so we grew up in each other's presence. We have a past, but what about a present? A future? I am injured to know what you say to others about me. To get them to distrust and dislike me. To get them to adore and pity you. These words ricochet back to me. It puts up another gate between us. What really ticks me off is that you mold me into the villain, and you the anti-hero desperate for justice. I realize you are an entertainer, that you captivate your audience with lies and twisted truths. I am not that easily manipulated though. You fooled me once, years ago. But never again. So you turn people against me to make yourself look better. To assist in your popularity. As if your race was with me only. Like you have to outdo me at everything in the world. You have to be smarter, more handsome, talented, and advanced. You even told me that you used me and my shortcomings in order to make yourself feel better and that it disturbed you to watch me evolve. How sad that is. That you can never be happy for me. That you only wish me misery. And then turn and call me your friend. Now I can admit, during…

**Star Boy (continued)**

…our entire friendship, I wasn't always mature or understanding. But I was also young and naïve. Things are different now and I don't want those kind of relations anymore. I haven't had the greatest friends. And maybe I wasn't always the greatest friend myself. But I can't waste any more time on these futile connections. Bonds that are a mockery of caring. I don't need another Lex Luthor. I don't want to be the guy you want to know about merely to placate your ego and go and spread the gossip. What's especially strange, is that you are telling people things about me that you are doing yourself. Making me out to be a horrible person while you go around doing worse things. Am I judging? No, it's your life. I am not concerned with your indiscretions and misadventures. I won't go and paint you the leper within a 200-mile radius. I won't try to sabotage every friendship or relationship that you will try to make. I won't warn people about you and your tainting ways. I won't try and force an opinion about you down other's throats. Because I am not like you. Because that is not what "real" friends do.

## imaginative seduction

Mr. him thinks:

Skin so vibrant, so tantalizing
Room's glance is sufficient enough
For heart stopping, blood pumping, fantasy starting
Want my breath in that long hair
On that small lobe under the ear
Around the back of the neck and back around
Eye to eye, mouth to mouth
Knocking on the door of serenity
Animal instinct kicking in overtime
A heated rush, a burning raging desire
Blistering the insides until contact
Cause contact is crucial here
To touch this fascinating flesh
Feel the moisture from within
Reveal all the hidden treasures
And thrust my daydream into reality
Together we can exercise for hours
Until the aching, sweaty, spent arms
Can no longer hold on
And we both fall limp with satisfaction

Miss Her thinks:

Eyes wander in his direction
What a beautiful man
Suddenly my thought process shifts
We would make out softly
Or he would jam his tongue down my throat…

**imaginative seduction** **(continued)**

…Either way I want it- I want it now
This sudden quivering sensation
Could take my hand to masturbation
As my mind plays pretend
Make believe is fun yet lacking
In comparison to my body touched
Touched by my lover in places of lustful sin
Exploring each part of our sexual nature
As two become one
Lips lock in passionate kiss
Sensual juices start to flow
Timid moans become loud groans
Fuck me for dinner
And again for breakfast
His sweet taste fulfills every urge inside me
My mind is screaming with excitement as I reach climax
But in reality my pussy still drips for his sex

they went opposite ways, never knowing....

(co-written by Jennifer Amanda)

**SEX SLAVE FOR A DAY:**

ok .....locked in a room 24 hours, my slave........ hmmm, let's see here.......well i think first i'd have you undress yourself, very very slowly......then i'd make you undress me...i'd tell you to stand up straight and be very very still...then i'd slowly breathe all over every part of your body, just teasing you....i would take some ice and rub on your breasts and let it drip down to your toes, then when you were good and wet i'd lick the water off your body..... then i'd tell you to sit down and i would watch as i commanded you to touch yourself, rubbing your tits and your clit until finally inserting your fingers inside yourself.....then i would came toward and get behind you and lick every inch of your body starting from back to front.......treating each area carefully....when i get to your mouth, i'd slip my tongue inside you and kiss you passionately, back and forth, your tongue and mine....i would kiss your neck and play-bite around, nibbling on your smooth skin......i would lick around your nipples and finally suck them as well...inch my way downward and tongue the clit for awhile....then lapping inside of you, feeling my way to your favorite spot.......then i turn the other way, and slip my cock in your mouth as i continue eating you out.... then i turn back to face you.....and slowly put myself inside you ......then we'd take turns switching up as many positions as we could think of......you on top, behind, standing up, sideways, etc......then just before cumming, i'd remove myself.........then blindfold you and the tie you up and then proceed to fuck you until you are screaming for more..... BUT HEY, THAT'S JUST THE FIRST HOUR..... then again, umm ..maybe we'd just talk all night, hmmm?..........

## Minimalist

The following story may appear horrendous and grotesque in nature, but what makes this horrid tale even grizzlier is that it is completely true:
Deep in the jungle soaked heart of the summer of 2007, having to minimally exist with little resources, I spent a total length of over 48 hours, over 2 whole excruciating days, without Myspace and without any new emails read. In fact, I had no internet connection and availability whatsoever. Not a small feat by any means. People wonder, "how did you do it?" Well, it was sheer stamina that propelled me forward. Forcing myself to survive through this dark and enduring time. After going into shock a few hours in, wondering if I had new blog or photo comments, I scavenged the barren terrain for something to occupy my time. I grabbed a dusty book off the shelf and began distracting myself from the internal craving. But the addiction ate away at me until I decided to go for a walk. Motion seemed to slow down the compulsion. My thoughts were scattered. From love to life to war to fear to hate to "I wonder if any new episodes of The Office has been uploaded and ready to watch?" Then the panic set in again. To divert the attack, I continued moving. Went to a local fast food eatery and got some ice cream then came back and watched some old home VHS tapes. Lulled to sleep by the poor sound quality but waking up in an icy sweat, coming to the realization that I'm bidding on an Ebay item that ended at midnight. "Did I win? Did I get outbid?" Uncertainty filled the air. I drank a tall glass of orange/mango juice and calmed my shaky nerves.

## Minimalist (continued)page2

The second day in, little hives had begun forming on my skin. I was in quite a delirium by now. Seeing mirages of Internet Explorer and Yahoo in my wake. The calluses on my fingertips were healing, softening from their inactivity. Pacing back and forth, listening to some old cassette tapes, I air-guitared my way through a few solemn hours. Inevitably though, I regressed. I speculated on what were the top 5 revolving stories on AOL? Stuck in these devastating trenches would I ever know? Tomorrow will be too late. I grabbed the phone in desperation.

Intending to call some random informant. After much struggling with my inner conscience, reasoning overtook me and my hand went limp, releasing the phone. The sky was turning dark again and a newfound hope surged through me. The knowledge that by this time tomorrow I would be online and everything would be ok. I will be admired and envied for my bravery and endurance. With night in full swing, began plucking my bass guitar, making halfway rhythmic sounds. I jogged a bit. And actually cleaned, a little. Dusting this, vacuuming that. My muscles were sore from performing so many actions and my head was spinning. I watched the Wishmaster but it only made me think of wishlist. My Amazon Wishlist. What if the prices have gone down? I gave in to the fact that I could very well lose a bargain out here in this prehistoric house without amenities.

## Minimalist (continued)page3

Finally the days had past. Loading up the car and preparing for the drive home, a serene calm washes over me, like a captive set free at last. The journey takes over 2 hours but I am steadfast in my convictions. Every time an ache singes me, I counteract with thoughts of blissful times, being just a click away. This grueling ride seemed to never end. Just when I feared an anxiety-induced breakdown, mere minutes from collapse, I pulled into the driveway. Running to the door, I flung my keys and darted toward the pious sanctity. With trembling hands, I turned the power on. Watched in eager anticipation for Windows to boot up. And at long last, the nightmare was over. Typing in "www.my" automatically showed "www.myspace.com/fauxpas23". With one click and a password, I was back in civilization.

It had been an unfortunate tragedy; one I hope you readers never have to suffer through. But I did. It was my biggest challenge, and I triumphed over this adversity and survived. A modern warrior of grandeur ready for the history books.

## On The Hunt

Silently I stalk around you
Watching you out of peripherals
Catch you doing mundane chores
You hear a noise and jump!
You think someone is there
No one is, just me
I inch closer without detection
You begin to hum a melody
Drowning out my approach
Slowly creeping toward you
In stealth mode, prepared to attack
Facing your backside
As you inadvertently clean
I lunge forward
Just as you turn around
You see me and shriek in panic!
What am I?
A ghost?
A killer?
A monster?
… I'm just a cat, silly.

## No Positive in Negatives

Going through old photo albums. Tracing the past with visual freeze frames. A haunted world existing only in the mind. Did any of this really happen? So far away, so far removed. Could easily be construed with a dream or work of fiction. Seeing how insane I was once upon a time. The clothes, the piercings, the hair, the attitude. Like a bizarro version. A skinny mutant trying to make a statement. Trying to find myself. See the pictures I took of you that time we had sex in the woods. Out in the open world for all to see. One guy did as I recall. See the drunken shots of my mutilation days. A dark period to say the least. Obsessed with dying and you. See you acting out in front of my car where I would pick you up from work. See all the scenes of playing music, the one thing that ever gave me a sense of purpose. All the waterfall shots from the high school days. We were kings. All the vacation photos, trips I took with you. My family, still alive and all together. My life spread out before me. Fills me with sadness. I try to look back and find the positives, but all I have are the pics, memories, and the negatives. No positive in the negatives.

## Mortal Wound

A wounded pup
Damaged goods
Wanting to crawl
Under a rock
And die
Wanting to escape
The prophecy
Wanting to surpass
Expectations
Dizzy from the hemorrhage
The mortal wound
That rips wider
Everyday
The chemical laboratory
Cursing the formulator
The baggage too heavy
To carry on board
The mother ship
The scar too deep
To ever heal
The wound
Seeping through the gauze

## Understudy

Body double
Stunt double
I want a life double
Someone to live my life
Out for me
I no longer want the job

Someone to say my lines
Mimic my moves
While I go incognito
Partying anonymously
Watch in third person
Every act of me

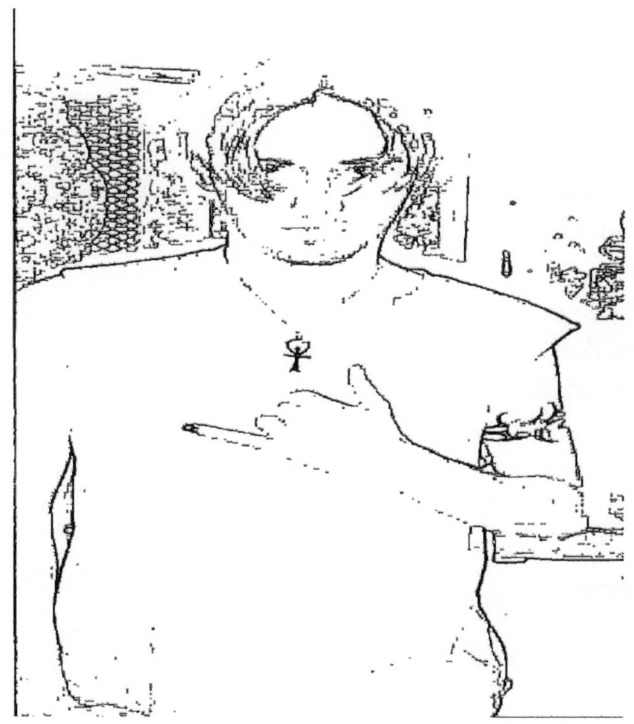

## Cliques and Crushes

Given sentiments
Folded notes
Borrowed jackets
Claddagh rings
Seductive smiles
Gentle nudges
Slow dances
Pulsing rush
New opportunity
New connection
Secret crushes
Forwardly revealed
Awkwardly stumble
First events
Each milestone
Love grows
Unlikely places
Brick jail
Learning structure
Cliques abound
Few mingle
Within sects
Smokers smoke
Geeks geek-out
Jocks jock
Lovers love
Sitting alone
I write
Passion poems
For you.

## Secret Wisdom

Looking for the secret of life?
Simple really
Find something
Conventional or un
Be it a person, place, object, idea, career, cult,
animal, sexual position, literature, film,
painting, song, or other blinding obsession
Just something. Find it
And enjoy it. Embrace it
Take it on the long subway ride
Fuck the worries and problems and bullshit
Fuck the drama and the blandness of the journey
Don't read some shitty pessimistic
poet writer who says "everything sucks"
Fuck him
What does he know?
It's your canvas
Paint it anyway you like
Stop looking for answers, reasons, and a big meaning
Just find some simple anchor
Some sense of purpose
Some destiny
And hopefully have fun fulfilling it.

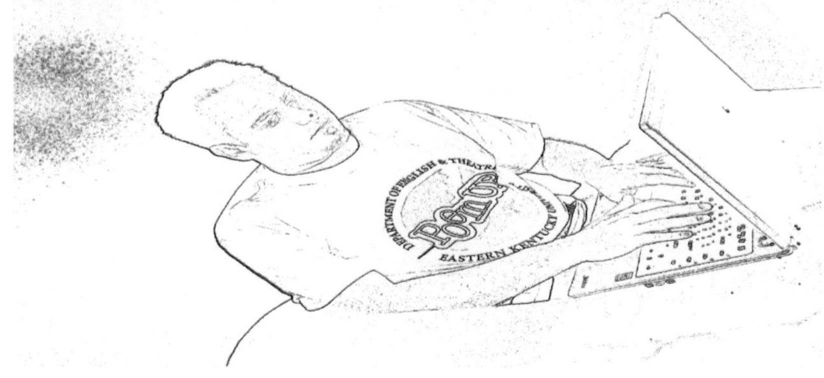

Michael Wade Johnson lives @ the KY/TN border and has been writing words "artistically" since the early 90's. He has many books: ***Poet's Journal, Misery Melodies & Dirty Dirges, Defining Love, Nymph's Denial, Pasty Pale Darkness****, and* ***Knight After The Reign*** originally under the pseudonym "Loser" Johnson. A title used primarily because no one else in the world would. He was a writer in ***the Virtual Chemists volume 1 & 2***, compiling and editing the second volume. He is also the compiler/editor of ***From A Common Spring vol. 1-3*** and the ***West Memphis Witch Hunt***. Most of his works can be found @ www.lulu.com/spotlight/micwjohnson. Find out more about Michael at www.facebook.com/Micwj. He is currently working on film projects, having written many screenplays. His company Faux Pas Films can be found @ www.imdb.com/company/co0281111/.

Thanks to:
Marcie, Jennifer Amanda, and Scott

PSYCHO

www.ingramcontent.com/pod-product-compliance
Ingram Content Group UK Ltd.
Pitfield, Milton Keynes, MK11 3LW, UK
UKHW041933190726
13854UKWH00004B/1569